A Gift For:

....

From:

....

Hallmark

Adapted from 1 Samuel 17

Copyright © 2017 Hallmark Licensing, LLC

Published by Hallmark Gift Books,
a division of Hallmark Cards, Inc.,
Kansas City, MO 64141
Visit us on the Web at Hallmark.com.

All rights reserved. No part of this publication
may be reproduced, transmitted, or stored in any
form or by any means without the prior written
permission of the publisher.

Editor: Kim Schworm Acosta
Editorial Director: Delia Berrigan
Art Director: Chris Opheim
Designer: Scott Swanson
Production Designer: Dan Horton

ISBN: 978-1-63059-753-5
1KDD1706

Made in China
0719

An ittybittys® Storybook

DAVID AND GOLIATH

BY ANDREW BLACKBURN ILLUSTRATED BY RALPH COSENTINO

**David was a boy who spent
a lot of time with sheep.
He gave them food. He kept them safe.
He sang them off to sleep.**

He lived a simple shepherd's life,
at home out on the range.
But little did he know
that life was all about to change.

Down the road from David
was a much less peaceful scene.
The Philistines had all arrived.
And they were being mean!

"I'm Goliath!" said Goliath.
"Send somebody out to fight me!
If I win, we'll take your land!
If not, we'll leave politely."

When David heard the news,
he headed straight to find King Saul.
"I'll fight Goliath," David said.
"I know I may be small.

"But guess what? God is on my side. I've got nothing to fear!"
"Great!" said Saul. "Go get 'em! You're our only volunteer."

"Before you fight the giant," said King Saul, "put on this gear. And take this sword. And hold this shield. And here's a nice long spear!"

"Um," said David, "thanks, but no.
I don't need all that stuff!
My trusty sling and these five stones
will be more than enough."

So David faced Goliath,
sling and stones his only tools.
"Ha! A child?" the giant said.
"What is this—April Fools'?"

"Not quite," said David.
"Though I'm glad you find it so amusing.
But God is on my side.
So I'm afraid I won't be losing."

Then David swung a stone
above his head inside the sling.
He held his breath, took careful aim,
then gave a mighty FLING!

His hand released the stone,
and it soared swiftly through the sky . . .
and then it struck Goliath
right between his giant eyes!

Goliath swayed from side to side,
then toppled to the ground.
It was silent for a moment.
Then cheers came from all around!

The army of the Philistines had turned around to run! And Israel all shouted out: "We won! We won! We won!"

"You did it, David!" said King Saul.
"Man, you were in the zone!"
"Hey, thanks!" said David.
"But I didn't do it on my own.

"I may have fought Goliath, but the victory is God's. And there's nothing He can't help us do— no matter what the odds."

If you enjoyed these itty bittys
and the story that they told,
then we would love to hear from you,
our readers young and old!

Please send your comments to:
Hallmark Book Feedback
P.O. Box 419034
Mail Drop 100
Kansas City, MO 64141

You can also write a review
at Hallmark.com,
or e-mail us at
booknotes@hallmark.com.